Hands On Literacy

BY

TRISH PETERSON, MS ED.

Bloomington, IN Milton Keynes, UK

AuthorHouse™
1663 Liberty Drive, Suite 200
Bloomington, IN 47403
www.authorhouse.com
Phone: 1-800-839-8640

AuthorHouse™ UK Ltd.
500 Avebury Boulevard
Central Milton Keynes, MK9 2BE
www.authorhouse.co.uk
Phone: 08001974150

First published by AuthorHouse 3/19/2007

ISBN: 978-1-4343-0128-4 (sc)

Library of Congress Control Number: 2007901619

Printed in the United States of America
Bloomington, Indiana

This book is printed on acid-free paper.

TABLE OF CONTENTS

CHAPTER ONE:

Characteristics of a Good Reader

The best indicator of a good reader is a child that is excited about learning and has a good language base. Children that come to school with language and an eagerness to learn are the ones most likely to succeed in reading. Contrary to what the toy industry is telling our society, the home environment contains all the opportunities necessary for language to grow. "Face to face contact with parents is critical. The baby must see you speaking so he can see, and hear how words are pronounced." The quantity of words the baby is exposed to correlates directly to his language development. "Only those words spoken directly to him count toward language development. Overhearing telephone conversations, words heard on the television including videotapes or DVDs is of no help to the child."

The building of a good language base occurs primarily through play. In the book Play and Literacy in Early Childhood Development, Kathleen Roskos has compiled research of 14 professors in early childhood. . Research consistently shows children that have spent the most time playing are the ones that have the easiest time learning to read All of the research comes to the same basic conclusion. The more children engage in imaginary play, the easier it is for them to learn to read. This is true for two basic reasons. When you read, you need to be able to picture in your head what is happening in the story. This ability to picture the story in your head is very important in comprehending what you read. The second element is the use of language. Children that are engaging in imaginary play are using their own words to create problems and solutions.

The industry of computerized stuffed animals, movies designed for children, and television shows are ignoring the process children should be taking to develop language. Children learn best through play, through interacting with their environment. Most early childhood experts agree that children need time to do nothing. The television and computer need to be turned off so the children can interact with the real world. The child needs to have a chance to play. With the majority of our children in childcare centers, parents need to make sure evenings or weekends are set aside as play time for their child. I realize this is easier said than done.

But it is important to realize that another component for a good reader is a good role model. We know that a child learns not based on what we say, but on what we do. This is as true for what children eat as well as whether children learn to read. Dr. Susan Kontos of Purdue University finds that the presence of adults engaged in literate behavior characterize homes of children who become successful readers and writers at an early age. Children in these homes also benefit from adult-child interactions centered on meaningful reading and writing (Play and Early Literacy, p.91)

One unique study points to an interesting finding from a graduate student. Dr. Daniels tells of a student doing research on the importance of parents listening to their children read when they arrived home. She picked deaf parents of hearing children and some hearing parents of hearing children. Since the deaf parents couldn't listen, she expected those children to struggle with reading. What she found was the opposite. She found that the hearing children of deaf parents were _better_ readers than the hearing children of hearing parents. This inspired Dr. Daniels to do more intense research on how sign can help hearing children become better readers. This research is the focus of Chapter Three.

Now that you know what a good reader spends a lot of time doing, how can you create a home that encourages your child to engage in play and develop an interest in reading later? This is the focus of Chapter Two.

Another question you may have is: What are those literate behaviors parents engage in? That depends on the age of your child. You want to have age appropriate activities for your child. You don't want activities that are too easy or too hard. I have divided the last chapters of the book into activities to promote reading readiness by age groups. The two year old chapter is designed for children ages 24 months-35 months. Remember all children learn at different rates. Do not be surprised if your two year old is ready for some three year old activities before he officially turns three. Do not be worried if your two year is not ready for some of the activities until he is almost three. Each child will grow at his own pace. As a teacher for 20 years, I now work in early intervention with children that have a delay. It has been my experience that most children who have a language delay may be delayed in other areas as well. Children that do not have a language delay, unless there is a physical disability, will rarely have a delay in other areas. As a result, I have only listed Language Milestones and Fine Motor Milestones for each age. I have included the fine motor because sign language is a fine motor activity. Approximations you see in sign are directly due to the fine motor skills of your child.

If you are concerned about your child's personal/social skills, his cognitive skills, or his motor skills, please call your county's department of social services and ask to have a core evaluation done on your child. Early intervention is a free service provided by your county to assess any child of a delay and to provide services to a delayed child so the parent knows how to help that child learn. I have seen many children with early intervention services catch up to their peers and go off to kindergarten with no noticeable delays. So getting early intervention involved with your child is a step I recommend to any parent worried about a delay or any parent interested in making sure there is no delay. The tests to see if your child is doing age appropriate tasks is free to anyone worried their child.

CHAPTER TWO:

Ways to Create a Reader Friendly Home

THINGS TO DO:

1. Have age appropriate books for your child. Be careful! Just because the book has been made into a board book does not mean it is a good book to have in your home. A list of good books from the American Library Association is listed in the back of the book for your use.

2. Separate the books from the toys. The best place to have the child's books is in his room. That way he can go to his bedroom and "read" whenever he wants.

3. When creating your daily routine, make sure reading a story to your child is part of that routine. Start small. Your average two year old will not sit and listen to a long story. Don't force your child to listen to a whole book. When you begin to read to your child, as he closes the book simply say, "The End." You should do this even if you have only read two pages. As his at-

tention span lengthens, you will have the opportunity to read the book when he is ready to listen.

4. Let your child know that a book is not a toy. Books are not things to be played with. Children as young as 18 months are capable of turning a board book correctly. Leave five books in a reading basket in his bedroom. One of those will be his favorite book. Keep that book in the basket. As you bring home new books, alternate the other books in the basket. If you have all the children's books together, your child will be overwhelmed. He will not be able to decide which book to look at so he will not look at any of them. That is why you will only have five books in his basket.

5. Have writing materials available. Children love to draw. You may want to begin with thick markers, and fat crayons. I know physical therapists that recommend children begin to color with broken small crayons. If the crayon is small, the child must use a correct grip to keep the crayon from falling out of his hand. So don't throw those broken crayons away.

6. Let your child see you read and write. The more he sees you enjoying a good book or writing a message, he will want to do the same. We are the role models for our children. Children see what their parents do for more hours in the day than anyone else. Parents need to show children that reading and writing are an important part of the adult world. Let your children watch you find a recipe in the cookbook, look up a friend's number in the phone book, or go to the library and use the card catalog. Detailed activities for your child's age begin with two year olds in Chapter Four.

CHAPTER THREE:

American Sign Language: My Child Isn't Deaf, Why Should I Sign?

In my fifteen years of teaching the deaf, I have worked with many deaf adults. I always brought them into my classroom. Since 90% of deaf children have hearing parents, most have only seen hearing adults. So they think they will be able to hear when they grow up. Since this is not true, I would invite deaf adults to come for a story hour with my students. It helped them understand there is a deaf culture, a deaf world that one day they will be a part of.

When talking with these deaf adults, they would often talk about their children. I would always ask if their children were having any trouble. The answer was always no. When asked to speak at a national conference on Signing for Literacy, I went to NTID (The National Technical Institute for the Deaf) to look in their volumes of research on using sign language in educational settings. All the research that has been done on CODAs (Children of Deaf Adults) goes into detail about the complex language these children are able to sign to their parents at a young age.

While an undergraduate student at Penn State, I helped Dr. Prinz with a research study on language acquisition. He took four different groups of pre-school children: 1) hearing children with hearing parents 2) hearing children with deaf parents 3) deaf children with hearing parents 4) deaf children with deaf parents. Each child was videotaped in a play session with their parents. All the language, either English or American Sign Language was recorded with a camcorder. A graduate student and myself were in charge of watching all the videotapes and making a written note of the language used by the parents and children. When Dr. Prinz compiled the data, what he found was that hearing children with deaf parents had the highest level of spoken and signed language followed closed by deaf children of deaf parents. His hypothesis was that the children with the highest language level would also have the easiest time learning to read. He followed these children two years later and found this to be the case. The best early readers were the hearing children of deaf parents. His hypothesis was that the captioner on the televisions in the deaf households was the reason the hearing children's reading level was so high. A captioner is a device that puts the written word of what is being said on the television in a line on the bottom of the tv screen. This lets the deaf people follow what is happening on a television show. The hearing children of these parents were seeing the written word corresponding with the spoken word every day as they watched the television. Not much was done with this 1982 research.

Dr. Daniels had a graduate student in Conneticut that basically found the same thing. She came to Dr. Daniels and explained that the hearing children of deaf parents were the best readers, but that made no sense. If they didn't have parents that could listen to them read, how did they become such fluent readers. Dr. Daniels agreed that the research did not make much sense. When she left the small college in Conneticut to go to Penn State to teach, she decided to attempt to do more indepth research to see if that was really true. In the early 1990s, Dr. Daniels began her research on using sign to promote hearing children's literacy. This was the same time that MRIs and Cat Scans enabled us to do brain research on live people. We now know what goes on in the brain as people read and as people sign. These two pieces of research are critical in understanding why you should sign with your child that can hear.

Most of you already know about signing with babies. Dr. Garcia pioneered the research on using American Sign Language to communicate with babies. When he began to work on the book, he was actually an interpreter. He would spend his day signing for deaf adults. They would invite him into their home. As he sat signing to the parents, he was amazed at how much language the young children could sign. Research shows his initial observation is correct. The average hearing child of deaf parents will begin to sign to their parents their first word at five months. At the age of nine months, they will be communicated in 2 word sentences and have a vocabulary of 50-75 signs. By contrast the average hearing child of hearing parents will say only one word by the age of twelve months, or one year old.

We have known about the terrible twos for along time. We all know that our child has something to say, cannot get it out, and has a "meltdown." Deaf parents, however, don't know what we are talking about. Their children do not have the temper tantrums associated with the terrible twos. Dr. Garcia began to wonder if the hearing parents would use sign language with their children, would the terrible twos go away? What he found was startling. Hearing children of hearing parents were able to communicate in sign the same as hearing children of deaf parents could. The temper tantrums were significantly reduced. One of the biggest concerns was a child talking. Since they were signing, would they bother to talk? Not only did they talk, they actually would talk sooner than hearing children that did not sign. The reason for that is obvious. Hearing children were putting sentences together in sign. When their tongues were finally coordinated to talk, they were able to speak in sentences. Why? Their brain was already wired to process sentences in sign so speaking in sentences came automatically.

Dr. Garcia's book Sign with Your Baby gives more detailed information on using sign with hearing children and about 100 words to use with your baby. If you haven't signed with your child yet, you should definitely purchase his book. It will give you a basic two year old vocabulary. There is a national network of presenters that offer sign language classes designed for parents with hearing children that would like to sign. To find if there is a class near you, go to www. sign2me.com. I offer classes in the NY/PA area. If there is not a Sign2Me class near you, most communities have a sign language class offered through Community Education or a college. It has become the second most popular foreign language in the United States after Spanish and is taught in high schools throughout the United States as a foreign language.

When you sign to your child, it is important that you only sign the important words, or the basic concept. For example, if you were asking, "Do you want some milk?", you would only sign milk and shrug your shoulders so your child knows a question is being asked.

Dr. Daniels feels this approach to incorporating sign into the spoken word is why it is so successful with literacy for hearing children. While a child is hearing a long sentence, he is seeing in sign what the important word/s in that sentence are. When a child is a very good reader, he will need to do the same thing. He will skip the words that have no meaning. When a good new reader begins a page, the first thing he will do is look at the picture on the page. This helps him know what the page is about and will help him with guessing any unfamiliar words. His eyes will go quickly over common words that are not important for meaning, the for example.

The boy is going to the store to buy milk for his mother. A good reader will read boy go store buy milk mother. The brain will add the extra words he needs for it to make sense in English. These are the same words that would be signed in ASL. While signs exist for words like the, is, to, for, they were invented by hearing teachers trying to help the deaf become better readers. Called SEE or Signed Exact English, the teachers felt if the deaf could see English all day, then they would become better readers. Unfortunately, after using SEE for 25 years in programs for deaf children, the reading level never improved. The average deaf high school graduate still reads at a fourth grade level. A new program based on ASL called Fairview Learning has started to be offered at schools for the deaf and some mainstreamed programs. In this program, children sign in ASL and change the written word to make a correct English sentence. Based primarily on ESL (English as a Second Language) research, Fairview Learning believes the deaf need to master their own language American Sign Language first and then be given a bridge between English and ASL.

If SEE did not work for deaf children learning to read, I would not advocate using it with your child either. Learn signs for the important words in the story. Do not sign every word.

Dr. Daniels went to inner city Philadelphia to do research on using sign language with hearing children. She had two Title IX kindergarten classrooms. Both had teachers that had taught kindergarten for a long time. Both groups were similar in ability. She taught one teacher signs for all the basic concepts she would cover that year. As the teacher taught, she would sign the important words. When introducing a letter, she would sign the letter. The teacher found signing in this arena very helpful. We are visual learners. As the teacher would hold up the letter written on a card, she could scan the room and see who had signed the letter correctly and who didn't know the letter yet. Without sign, she would never be sure who was lost. Which child had their mouth open but was saying nothing? Which child was saying the wrong letter? The teacher didn't know. Since each child was given her the manual alphabet she was able to see how successful each child was before trouble appeared on a written test.

Dr. Daniels performed a pre-test in the Fall and a post-test in the Spring. When she tested the children in the Fall, both groups were at the same level. When she tested the children in the Spring, the children in the signing classroom were at or above grade level. The children in the classroom that did not sign were slightly delayed. Five years later, Dr. Daniels returned to Philadelphia to see how these students were doing. Normally in Title IX classrooms, students excel when they receive the small group instruction in kindergarten and first grade. By third grade, they begin to fall behind again and remain behind the rest of their school days. What she found was the students in the classroom where signing had been used in kindergarten were still at or above grade level. Signing for only kindergarten was able to put these children on par with their peers and give them the foundation they needed to be successful.

Research is finally showing children that sign are successful in reading because Broca's area of the frontal lobe controls skillful movements of the hands, the kind of movement used to produce sign language or the manual alphabet. (4, p.126) Kindergarten teachers have known that finger movements are essential to learning for a long time. That is why so many use finger plays to help children create a hand link. While that may work for kindergarten, when the children move on to more abstract concepts, the finger plays don't really work anymore. The signs they have learned, however, can continue to help them incorporate their hands into learning.

CHAPTER FOUR:

Activities to Promote Reading Readiness

2-3 YEAR OLDS

The language explosion has begun. By 18 months, children say about 50 words. Between 18-20 months, your child can learn as many as 9 new words a day. They begin to combine words into sentences and ask never ending questions about the world around them. (3)

By the time he reaches 31-36 moths, he will be having conversations. He will be asking and answering who where and when questions and will be using prepositions (on, under, over, etc.) in his sentences(6).

According to Bell, both the hand and eye develop as sense organs through practice as the brain teaches itself by making the hand and eye learn to work together. (4, p.130) Involving the hands in the reading process, makes it easier for the brain to process the written word. Sign Language is a perfect way to involve the hand in language development.

A parent, Jennifer, reports, " Eliana has been interested in the alphabet for quite some time now, this interest has recently reached a new level. She goes around signing letters all the time and takes great pride in telling you what letter a particular word starts with (without being told). It really started a few weeks ago while we had some friends over, one of whom is named Tim. Eliana proudly exclaimed out of nowhere, 'T! Tim!" while showing us the sign for "t". She now signs t,m for Tim and also enjoys trying to sign other names, not the least of which is her own. I just find it fascinating that she's making this connection with phonics and trying to spell at the age of 2! I'm totally convinced that signing has played a major part in this development. It's so wonderful to help unlock some of her potential!"

Jennifer is just one of many parents that have experienced an increase in phonics, word decoding because the child has been exposed to sign language. Your toddler is a natural explorer. This curiosity helps language develop. He will listen to adults, he loves listening to stories. By listening to the same story repeatedly, your toddler learns about the way stories are created. This will help him when it comes time to be a reader or writer.

You can help your toddler become a reader and writer by incorporating talking and reading into every day activities. When you sign to this age child, sign the main idea of what you are saying. If you are talking about your trip to the grocery store, sign food and store. When you are at the store, ask the child what he would like and show him the signs for his favorite foods if he doesn't know them yet.

Don't forget about writing. Reading and writing are two different parts of the same process. Try to write words down with your children to show them these two activites (reading and writing) are connected parts of the same process (5, p.12)

Remember it is not polite to talk with your mouth full, but you can sign with your mouth full!

When reading a book to your child, do not sign every word. Pick a few words on each page to sign to your child. At first pick the pictures to sign. Later when he can sign all the pictures, you can add other important words in the story.

LANGUAGE MILESTONES

Follows 2-3 component command

Ex: Go to your bedroom and bring me a diaper (2 component)
Ex: Go to the living room, pick up your teddy bear and put it
  away (3 Component)

Recognizes and identifies almost all common objects and pictures
(Can point to the cow, pig, etc upon request)

Understands most sentences
Understands physical relationships (On, in, under)
Uses 4-5 word sentences
Can say name, age and sex (boy or girl)
Uses pronouns and some plurals
Strangers can understand most of his words.

LANGUAGE ACTIVITIES:
HIDE AND SEEK

Change the traditional hide and seek to the hiding of stuffed animals.

After you hide the animal, let the child begin to search. Do not use the single words like hot and cold; instead, use prepositional phrases.

Examples: The animal is in the living room. If the child is unable to find where in the living room it is, give him more specific hints. It is under the couch. If the child finds where in the living room it is, ask questions. Where did you find the cat?

If the child responds, "in the living room.", give her more language.

"Yes, you found it in the living room under the couch. Good job. Now it is your turn to hide the cat."

Children love this game. Make sure to include hiding places that use the following prepositions: in, on, under, behind, beside, on top of, and next to.

Pretend the animal is sleeping and you don't want to wake him up. Give all your clues in sign language and have the child ask questions like that too. Children love this game!

GROCERY LIST

Make a shopping list with your child. As he tells you what he would like, let him watch you add it to the list. Give him a piece of paper to help create his own list if he asks. When you take it to the store, let the child see you reading the list and crossing things off as you find them. This lets him know that words have a purpose.

QUIET TIME

Have books for the child under 6 years old that are based on reality rather than fantasy. Keep only a few at a time in a small basket in his bedroom. Never mix books with toys…We should teach children from the beginning to handle books with care, turning the pages from the top. Separating the books from the toys, lets the child know that books are not toys. Books are something different. Since children at this age love to imitate, it is important that they see you reading for pleasure.

During this age, your child will begin to outgrow his nap time. I strongly suggest you keep this time and call it Quiet Time. He is required to go to his bedroom with his basket of books. He can sleep or look at his books. If he has a basket of books, you can place it on his bed. This will let him lay and read or sleep. By keeping toys out of the child's bedroom, you are letting him know that his bedroom is for sleeping, reading, or other quiet activities. Do not be surprised if you see your child looking through his books, pointing and signing all the pictures he knows.

Some parents find calming music helpful during quiet time. Try to use instrumental music only so the child can concentrate on the pictures and words that go with the books and not the words of the songs.

FINGER ACTIVITES
PLAY DOUGH

Letting the children create things with play dough is good for strengthening the muscles of the fingers needed for writing. All the child needs is the play dough and someone to show him how to play. He needs to see you roll the play dough with your hand and make balls, ducks, spiders, trucks, or whatever your imagination would like to create.

Try to avoid the pre-made play dough kits. This limits the child's imagination to only the specific category of the kit. Remember children should always be exposed to real situations first so avoid the fictional characters in play. It is amazing the world your child will create with play dough. Be sure to have a large counter top or table for him to use.

Letters

As you walk around the block with your child, point to the letters you see. As you point to the letter, show him how you sign that letter. Pick one letter for each word. The Stop Sign for example, you might first show him the letter S. Later when he is already signing S, you can introduce another letter he doesn't know yet. This lets him see that words are comprised of letters. As you read to him, let him find all the S on a page before you turn to the next part of the story.

As you are getting boxes of food out to cook dinner, read the labels to him. Show him the first letter and sign it for him. If there is an S in the name also, show it to him. Soon he will realize words are composed of letters and point to the letters he knows everywhere he sees them.

Teaching him the first letter of his name is also fun. Children at this age love to see their name in print. If you have a relative that lives far away, encourage them to write to your child. Seeing a letter arrive in the mail from someone with his name on it, is very exciting at this age. After reading the letter, ask the child to dictate a letter back. As he talks, you can type or write. When he is finished, you can write his name on the bottom. If he would like to try to write his name, let him try the first letter. Show him the steps to writing that letter. Create a dotted line of the correct letter and let him trace it.

THINKING OF A WORD GAME

By Suzanne DeCredico www.babychatt.com

I'm thinking of a word it rhymes with _____ (say and sign the word SWING for example) but starts with _____(sign the letter or letter combination while making the sound)
Later stop saying the word and letter, just sign them. This is great to play at the park. Just look around you to get ideas for words. This also works when stuck in a line at the store.

VARIATION: MAKING UP A SILLY WORD

"I'm making a silly word. It rhymes with _____
(Swing for example) but starts with _____.

Do the same as above. Start by saying and signing the word and letter or letter combination. Later do the word and new starting letter in sign only.

Start with basic letters b,d,f,g,h,j,k,l,m,n,p,r,s,t,v,w,z

Notice I skipped the letter c. It only makes either an s or a k sound. Q is really a KW sound so I skipped it as well. Vowels will not create a rhyming word.

WHERE IS _____ (LETTER)?

Kids love looking for the mouse in Goodnight Moon. Have the child search for a letter as you read your bedtime story. This is also fun to do with a magazine. You can take the big ad pictures, rip them out and let your child find and circle the letters. Since the ad only has a few words, the letter you said will be easy to find.

Make sure he knows that magazines or newspapers are things we throw away so we can write on them. We do not throw away books, so we cannot write in them. Instead, we will point to the letters in the book.

ANIMAL AND LETTER THUMBKIN

Children are quite young when they are able to distinguish between the name of an animal and the sound an animal makes (Daniels, p.19) Young children can learn that letters have names and letters make sounds just like the animals! Letters and animals both make different sounds in different situations. The cat says "purr" when you pet her bust says "hiss" when the dog comes too close. Sometimes, the cat is even totally quiet. Letters also make different sounds depending on which other letters are close to them. Sometimes letters don't make any sound at all.

This fun "Where is Thumbkin?" finger game uses animals, letters and signs while building the connections between the letters and letter sounds! Start with your hands behind your back. Make the animal come alive by signing when you say the word and when you make the animal sound.

Where is Lion?
Where is Lion?
Here I am (sign LION)
Here I am (sign LION)
What do you say lion? (sign LION)
What do you say lion (sign LION)
ROAR!!

Repeat with all the animals your children love.

You can also do this song with letters. I suggest you begin by the first letter of your child's first name. The second letter should be the first letter of your last name. Don't be surprised if your child has letters they would like to see next. This is the perfect way to introduce how to sign the alphabet to your child.

Where is F?
Where is F?
Here I am (sign F)
Here I am (sign F with other hand)

What do you say F?
What do you say F?
Fff,fff,fff
Fff,fff,fff

CHAPTER FIVE:

Activites to Promote
Reading Readiness

3-4 YEAR OLDS

From 37-42 months, he will talk clearly, use plurals, use the and a, and master songs and nursery rhymes (6). From 43-48 months, he will begin imagining, enjoying story time, and begin to make up words. He can finally express his feelings and loves to create silly rhyming phrases, ex. Anna Banana Fe Fi Fo Fanna Anna

He is learning about how things work in the world and his place in it. He is able to use an very growing vocabulary to share what he sees, learns, and imagines. He loves to share in conversations with you. He loves to create stories and pretend. Give him time to play in his own little world. Imaginary play is very important. When you read, you need to be able to picture what is going on in the book in your head. Children develop their imagination during play.

He becomes aware of letters in his world. He will begin to recognize words he sees often like McDonald's, Pizza Hut, stop, and his own name in print.

Many so-called early learning programs interfere with the child's natural enthusiasm by forcing him to concentrate on tasks for which he is not yet ready. (7,p.349) Try to keep the activities age appropriate and fun!

LANGUAGE MILESTONES

Understands same and different
Mastered the basic rules of grammar

Ex: He longer says Dad goed to work. Instead he says Dad went
to work.

Speaks 5-6 word sentences
A Stranger can understand everything he says
He tells stories

LANGUAGE ACTIVITIES
STORY TIME

Children are now ready for longer stories. Pick stories with
interesting plots and compelling characters. Fairy Tales are popular
with this age group. If you have a story hour at your library, take
your child. Going to the library to listen to a book and get to pick
books to take home are a fun activity for this age.

Children this age begin to recognize rhymes. Dr. Seuss' books are
filled with nonsense words that rhyme. This age loves to hear those
books again and again. Listening to these rhymes and rhythms is an
important step in developing an awareness of sounds. Another good
source is Mother Goose Nursery Rhymes.

RHYMING WORDS

Children this age enjoy making lists of words that rhyme. This
is perfect for when you are in the car. Begin by saying a small two
letter word: in, at, up for example. See how many works your child
can create that end with those letters. Accept silly words like hin or
zin.

Once you have finished the easy words, start with silly nonsense
words like jair and see if your child can find real rhyming words: air,
chair, hair, lair, fair

Feel free to use two syllable words like pitten for your child to create kitten, mitten. Make sure you only replace the first letter for now.

I See Something You Don't See and It is....

This game is a fun thing to play on a pretty day in your backyard or in your playroom on a rainy day. You can go first and pick something very big and obvious. All you tell your child about the object is its color. I see something you don't see and it is green. The child then can begin to guess what it is or can ask yes no questions. Is it outside? Is it near?

Once you have played a few times with big obvious objects, try smaller things. Make sure your child gets a turn to pick something and answer questions,too.

Fingerspelling Fun

By Suzanne De Credico (www.babychatt.com)
Fingerspell a short vowel word for your child. Have your child:

1. Show you the sign (ex: Cat, hat, big, fun,etc.)
2. Do the word (ex: run, sit, hop, read, kiss, tap, etc.)
3. Sign if he likes or doesn't like it (ex: egg, ham, red, pig, etc.)
4. Makes the sound (ex: buzz, pop, hiss, zapp)

Clouds

Another fun game to play is to sit and look at the clouds. See how many things you can find living in the clouds. It is amazing all the animals children see in the clouds that we adults do not see.

SHOPPING

Continue using a shopping list. Now let your child begin to "read" from the list. If he has shopped with you every week, he has repeatedly seen your favorite foods on the list now. This repetition is getting really boring for you, but it is very exciting for him. Repetition is how children learn. Point to the word on the list as you find it. Show him the label on the bottle or box and how it matches what you have written. If you have written mac and cheese and you buy Kraft Macaroni and Cheese, let him know that mac is a shortened way to write macaroni. Kraft is not written because it is the brand name we always buy so we don't need to write that down.

As you are going through the aisles, pick a letter of the day. See how many different labels you can find that have a word that starts with that letter. Show him that letter in sign. Go ahead and share the signs for the words he finds. Many signs in ASL begin with the same handshape as the letter they start with. For example, noodle is signed with the letter N handshape. A more comprehensive list of words that use the first letter of their English word are in the back of the book.

If you don't know the signs for the words he has found, write them on the back of your shopping list and look them up when you get home. A list of good sign language dictionaries and websites are listed in the back of the book.

Continue playing the rhyming game from the previous chapter. Use this for both the pretend and real rhyming words games. Your child will probably enjoy the silly words more at this age.

When your child has mastered the easy words, move on to blends.

Bl	br	ch	cl	cr	dr	fl	fr	gl	gr
pl	pr	sc	scr	sh	shr	sk	sl	sm	sn
sp	spl	spr	squ	st	str	sw	th	thr	tr

Continue finding letters in magazines and newspapers. Now start looking for letters in short articles or comic strips. Have a letter of the day and ask him to show you every time he sees that letter. It doesn't matter if it is on the cereal box at breakfast, in the newspaper, his favorite book, or written on a sign at the store.

WHERE IS THE LITTLE WORD?

By Suzanne DeCredico (www.babychatt.com)
Fingerspell and sound out these common two letter words: up, in, is, it, if, an, am, as and at. As you read a story, stop when you get to any of these words and have the child read that word. In no time, he will reading all these little words.

CHAPTER SIX:

Activities to Promote Reading Readiness

4-5 YEAR OLDS

LANGUAGE MILESTONES

1. Recalls part of a story
2. Speaks sentences of more than 5 words
3. Uses future tense
4. Tells longer stories
5. Says his name and address
   (7,p.347)

HAND AND FINGER MILESTONES

1. Copies triangle
2. Draws a person with a body
3. Prints some letters
4. Dresses/undresses without help
5. Uses fork and spoon
6. Cares for one toilet needs

Language Activities, Ages 4-5
Alphabet Soup

By Carol Carnley, MS CCC-SLP
S.O.S. Signs-Optimize-Speech

Variation One:

Provide alphabet crackers, cookies or soup for your child. The child will scoop up the letter with his spoon and then sign it to mom or dad. He must sign the letter to eat it. If mom or dad has to help model the letter, then the cracker or soup is shared. When the child is finished, it is the mom or dad's turn. This way your child gets a chance to learn a few letters by watching you.

You can add the sound this letter makes to begin awareness of sounds. Some parents like to add it while they are learning the alphabet without holding the child accountable. The parents that have tried this are amazed. By the time the child has mastered the manual alphabet, he has also mastered the majority of the sounds those letters make.

VARIATION TWO:

Mom or dad can fingerspell single letters or 2-4 letter words depending on the child's skill level while sitting in a restaurant, plane, waiting in line at the store,etc. The child tried to identify the fingerspelled letter or word. He earn 2 points if the target is named within 2 attempts of seeing the letter or word spelled. One point is eared on the third attempt. You decide how far play will continue (10 points,etc) as well as the prize. Start with a short game to keep the child interested. Keep a pad of paper and pencil to record points and to assist the game by writing down the named letters to aid the child in seeing the letters written on paper in addition to finger-spelled. This also helps you remember which letters or words have already been done in case the line is long.

If at the restaurant, the winner of the game maybe can get a dessert, or pick the toppings on the pizza,etc. At the grocery story, the child may choose one of three possible choices for a treat or special snack.

This activity is a great productive way to pass the time when you'd otherwise be doing nothing. This task promotes turn taking, phonetics, and it can be varied depending on your child's skill level.

I SPY, ADVANCED TASK

Have the child pick a favorite story or picture book. Buy an inexpensive magnifying glass and a pad of paper and pencil. The child is the detective and must collect the clues (ex. Green, jump, wet). Before he starts, you will give him the category (animal).

Look in the story book to narrow down the words that he could guess. If needed, fingerspell the first letter. If the child guesses frog, then he has to try to fingerspell it. I found it easy to create the clue cards from his favorite book while he was napping. When he awoke from his nap, I would have the first set of words already hidden. When he solved that mystery, I would give him the book to look at for ideas of what the next word might be. He would look at the book in one room while I hid the next set of words in other rooms.

My Book

While you go on a trip, take pictures. The next day, sit with your child, look at the pictures and create a book. Leave the top of the page empty so that he can draw what happened beside the picture if he'd like.

He will be the author of the story. As he looks at the pictures, ask him what happened and use his answers to create the story. Have him create the title for the story and put his name as the author. Read the book to him when you are done. Let him try to read the book too. It is a fun way to remember vacations you have had as a family.

List of Rooms

Ask your child to help you write about the rooms in your home. Follow the format
We_____in the _____.
Example: We cook in the kitchen.

Once you have written the first one, let your child try to copy the We in the for the next sentence while you fill in their new idea. You can have more than one idea for the same room.

Write a Letter

Sit with your child and write someone you both know a letter. Maybe you have a grandmother or aunt that lives far away. You could even write to dad and mail it to his work. Even if your grandmother lives nearby, you can still write a letter and mail it. This is a good activity to do after a busy day. The following day, have the child tell you what happened and you write the letter about what you did and mail the letter. When you are finished writing the letter, point to the words as you read the letter. Leave a big space between Sincerely and his name so that he can try to copy it. Don't erase or criticize his writing. Just send it off. Each time he writes his name, he will get closer and closer to doing it correctly.

VOWEL THUMBKIN

Play this game the same way as the animal and letter Thumbkin from the last chapter. The only difference is that a vowel has several different sounds it can make. Begin by introducing the short vowel sounds. When your child knows all the short vowel sounds, you can begin to change the melody of the song to include long and short vowel sounds. I have given both examples below. For the long a sound as found in words like ate, I have typed A. For the short a sound found in words like apple, I have typed aa.

Short vowel
Where is short A?
Where is short A?
Here I am (sign A)
Here I am (Sign A)
What do you say
    short A?
What do you say
    short A?
Aa,aa,aa
Aa,aa,aa

Both
Where is A?
Where is A?
Here I am (Sign A)
Here I am (Sign A)
What do you say A?
What do you say A?
Aa, A, aa
aa, A, aa

Long Vowel
Where is long A?
Where is long A?
Here I am (Sign A)
Here I am (Sign A)
What do you say
    long A?
What do you say
    long A?
A, A,A
A, A, A

Many words in American Sign Language use the handshape of the letter they start with to make the sign. Some examples are listed below.

A: attitude, area, aunt
B: brown, blue, bee
C: class, character, cop, cloud
D: dolphin, dessert, dream
E: elevator, Easter
F: French fries, France, Friday
G: guilty, green
H: hospital, hurry
I: Israel, idea
J: jelly, jealous
K: kangaroo, kitchen
L: library, lazy
M: Monday
N: niece, nephew
O: octopus, orange
P: party, purple, pink
Q: quilt, queen
R: ready, restroom
S: Saturday, Seattle
T: toilet, Tuesday
U: uncle
V: vanilla
W: Wednesday, water
X: X-ray
Y: yellow, yarn, yo yo
Z: Zoo

CHAPTER SEVEN:

Resources

BOOKS TO GROW ON

Printed by Permission of the ASLC

0-6 MONTHS

All Fall Down by Helen Oxenburg. Little Simon, 1999

Animal Crackers: Bedtime by Jane Dyer. Little, Brown, 1998

Baby Animals: Black and White Tides, by Phyllis L. Charlesbridge, 1998

Baby Rock, Baby Roll by Stella Blackstone. Holiday House, 1997

Big Fat Hen by Keith Baker. Harcourt, 1994.

Black on White by Tana Hoban. Greenwillow, 1993.

Blue Hat, Green Hat by Sandra Boynton. Little Simon, 1984.

How a Baby Grows by Nola Buck. Harper Collins, 1998.

Max by Ken Wilson-Max. Jump at the Sun, 1998.

My First Baby Games by Jane Manning. Harper Collins, 2001.

My Very First Mother Goose by Iona Opie. Candlewick, 1996.

6-12 MONTHS

Animal Kisses by Barney Saltzberg. Red Wagon, 2000.

Baby's Lap Book by Kay Chorao. Dutton,1991.

Brown Sugar Babies by Charles Smith. Jump at the Sun, 2000.

Goodnight Moon by Margaret Wise Brown. Harper Collins, 1947.

I Can by Helen Oxenbury. Candlewick, 1995.

I Smell Honey by Andrea Pinkney. Red Wagon, 1997.

Maybe, My Baby by Irene O'Book. Harper Collins, 1998.

My Colors (Mis Colores) by Rebecca Emberly. Little, Brown, 2000.

Red, Blue, Yellow Shoe by Tana Hoban. Greenwillow, 1986.

Time for Bed by Mem Fox. Harcourt, 1993.

Twinkle Twinkle Little Star by Jeannette Winter. Red Wagon, 2000.

Welcome Baby! Baby Rhymes for Baby Times by Stephanie Calmenson. Harper Collins,2002.

Where's the Baby? By Tom Paxton. Morrow Avon, 1993.

12-18 Months

The Bear Went Over the Mountain by Rosemary Wells. Scholastic, 1998.

Big Dog, Little Dog by Dav Pilkey. Harcourt, 1997.

Count with Maisy by Lucy Cousins. Candlewick, 1997.

Eating the Alphabet:Fruits and Vegetables from A to Z by Lois Ehlert. Harcourt, 1989.

The Everything Book by Denise Fleming. Henry Holt, 2000.

Five Little Monkeys Jumping on the Bed by Eileen Christelow. Clarion, 1989.

Freight Train by Donald Crews. Greenwillow, 1978.

Itsy Bitsy Spider by Rosemary Wells. Scholastic,1978.

Jamberry by Bruce Degen. Harper Collins, 1992.

My First Action Rhymes Pictures by Lynne Cravath. Harper Collins, 2000.

Pat the Bunny by Dorothy Kunhardt. Golden, 1942.

Rabbit's Bedtime by Nancy Elizabeth Wallace, Houghton Mifflin, 1999.

Read to Your Bunny by Rosemary Wells. Scholastic,1997.

Sheep in a Jeep by Nancy Shaw. Houghton Mifflin, 1986.

Ten, Nine, Eight by Molly Garrett Bang. Greenwillow, 1983.

Tom and Pippo Read a Story by Helen Oxenbury. Simon and Shuster, 1998.

Where is My Baby? By Harriet Ziefert and Simms Taback. Handprint, 2002.

Where's Spot? By Eric Hill. G.P.Putnam, 1980.

You are My Perfect Baby by Joyce Carol Thomas. Joanna Cotler, 1999.

Zoom City by Thatcher Hurd. Harper Collins, 1998.

18 MONTHS- 3 YEARS OLD

Be Gentle! By Virginia Miller. Candlewick, 1999.

Book! By Christine O'Connell George. Clarion, 2001.

Brown Bear, Brown Bear What Do You See? By Bill Martin, Jr. and Eric Carle. Henry Holt, 1992.

Chicka Chicka Boom Boom by Bill Martin and John Atchambault. Little Simon, 1989.

Color Zoo by Lois Ehlert. Harper Collins, 1989.

Come Along, Daisy! By Jane Simmons. Little, Brown, 1998.

Construction Zone by Tana Hoban. Greenwillow, 1997.

Dinosaur Roar! By Paul and Henrietta Strickland. Dutton, 1994.

Dinosaurs, Dinosaurs by Byron Barton. Harper Collins, 1989.

Hello, Lulu by Caroline Uff. Walker, 1999.

How Do Dinosaurs Say Good Night? By Jane Yolen. Blue Sky, 2000.

In the Tall, Tall Grass by Denise Fleming. Henry Holt, 1991.

Jesse Bear, What Will You Wear? By Nancy White Carlstrom. Simon and Schuster, 1986.

Little White Duck by Bernard Zaritsky and Walt Whippo. Little, Brown, 2000.

Maisy's ABC by Lucy Cousins. Candlewick, 1995.

"More More More" Said the Baby by Vera Williams. Greenwillow, 1990.

Mouse Mess by Linnea A. Riley. Scholastic, 1997.

On Mother's Lap by Ann Herbert Scott. Clarion, 1992.

Silly Little Goose! By Nancy Tafuri. Scholastic, 2001.

The Tale of Peter Rabbit by Beatrix Potter. Warne, 1999.

The Very Hungry Caterpillar by Eric Carle. Philomel, 1981.

The Wheels on the Bus by Raffi. Harper Collins, 1998.

SIGN LANGUAGE DICTIONARIES

Teach Your Tot to Sign by Stacy Thompson

This dictionary has a lot of common words children use that are hard to find in other sign language dictionaries, like puzzle and blocks.

www.handspeak.com

There is a small fee associated with this site, but it was created by deaf people and is very comprehensive. When you pay the small fee to join, you can type in the word and a deaf person will appear on your tv screen and sign the word for you.

www.signwithsam.com

This is a free site with pictures of signs for thematic words. A good way to print how to sign words for your favorite times of year and share them with friends.

American Sign Language Dictionary by Martin Sternberg

Small paperback dictionary will give you the most frequently used words. The big version will give you the most comprehensive list of signs found anywhere.

Signing with Hearing Children Resource Books

Dennis, Kirsten and Azpiri, Tressa, Sign to Learn: American Sign Language in the Early Childhood Classroom, c.2005

Garcia, Joseph Sign with Your Baby, c. 1999-2006.

Daniels, Marilyn Dancing with Words: Using Sign to Promote Hearing Children's Literacy, c.2002.